TOD BROWNING LOOSE-LEAF ENCYCLOPEDIA

THOMAS E. SIMMONS

TABLE OF CONTENTS

5

To David John Skal and Daniel Pratt Mannix IV,
popular culture commentator extraordinaire and
peerless sideshow performer, respectively (and
respectfully)

Introduction to Tod Browning

Browning directed *Dracula*
and so, if you know of him

that's how

     no doubt

Some put "direct" in quotes when
they speak of his "work" on *Dracula*

i.e., He 'directed' *Dracula.*

He (Browning, not the Count)
was born in Louisville

Later
     he died
         in Malibu

In the dash between the years
1880?-1962
he lived

This modestly
robust band
of verselets
sets its sights
on presenting
a few revolving
circus rings of Browning (cue: circus band)

with a foray or two
into poorly lit places –

meetings –
& a meal or two

littered with his creations (the ones he directed)
which –

in turn –

are littered with animalized
protagonists

(such Black Bird, Tiger, and
Cock Robin)

situated in a beguiling
hobgoblin-ary –

as well as several
biographical items of interest

Step right up
                    "Behold"

A Browning Background

The titles of the films that he directed,
wrote, or starred in, read like chants –

They command:

> *Dollar Down*
> *Hands Up!*
> *Set Free*

They question:

> *What's Your Husband Doing?*
> *Which Woman?*

They assert:

> *Everybody's Doing It*
> *Payment Guaranteed*
> *Music Hath Charms*
> *No Woman Knows*
> *After Her Dough*
> *Foiled Again*

They locate:

> *London After Midnight*
> *The Road to Mandalay*
> *Passion's Playground*
> *Out Again – In Again*
> *Where East is East*
> *Under Two Flags*
> *West of Zanzibar*

Outside the Law
Inside Job

Often, they introduce a character:

The Woman who Walked Alone
The Queen of the Band
The Man Under Cover
The Dangerous Flirt
The Exquisite Thief
The Brazen Beauty
The Incorrigible
Ethel's Teacher
A Fallen Hero
The Wise Kid
The Mascot
The Mystic

But mostly they just
proclaim their subject:

The Mystery of the Leaping Fish
The White Slaver Catchers
The Petal on the Current
The Fatal Glass of Beer
The Spell of the Poppy
The Face in the Dark
The Pointing Finger
The Lucky Transfer
The Electric Alarm
The Deciding Kiss
The Burned Hand
The Living Death

A Corner in Hats
The Willow Tree
The Jury of Fate
The 13th Chair
The Big City
Pink Tights
Parentage
The Show
Revenge
Freaks

Prelude to Vaudeville

When Tod Browning fingered
the mingy sprocket holes
of the silver nitrate films
inside the dented cannisters –

each image clocked to
a second's sliver
frozen in his hands

but spooling when the reels spun

Clackity-clack / clackity-clack –

he was fingering
his life's work
or most of it

But there was a childhood there too
and a vaudeville which preceded all

of that filmmaking
which we ought to flatter
with our attention
meriting it –
or granting it –
its own space

Here

Now

[insert 'moment of silence' title card for 3
beats]

Meanwhile, there were childhoods happening across
America

Too many, quite honestly, to fit into print

So just close your eyes for a moment

You do the imagining

Clackity-clack / clackity-clack

The Devil Doll (1936)

Setting:

Paris (1915)

Props:

Mind control, dreams formed in a dungeon
Loose cotton, resentment, filthy laundry
Iodine, orange extract, breadcrumbs
Very *very* tiny knives
Stiletto Apache doll
Beings without will
An escaped banker
Suitable harnesses
A halfwit maiden

Characters:

· Lionel Barrymore – 'The man of 2 faces'
· What can be stolen from a person
· Washed-out Cinderella(s)
· Gluepots in the alley

Premises:

1. All things are made of atoms
2. Atoms are made of electrons
3. You'll blow yourself to atoms
4. Protagonist does that (offscreen)

Theme:

 Whether the reduction of men is even
necessary

Resolution:

 Atoms descend the Eifel tower elevator @
sunset

Credits:

 [omitted]

White Tiger Trailer (1923)

TITLE SEQUENCE:

Behind the fog, we imagine that we hear the stirring of a skillet of red beans on a wood stove.

                              TOTAL DARKNESS:

FADE UP; ON
INT. RUSTIC CABIN – NIGHT

ENTER: Mike Donovan going under the name "Bill Hawkes" –

                 A stool pigeon.
                 A wolf.

CUT TO: A vague feeling – not of distrust – but of presentiment.

FADE TO: Collective distrust fueled by days-without-sleep.

                 Double-crosses collapsed on maze-wariness, heaped.

FADE UP TO: Sylvia (still in her evening wear) irritably stirring a pot-of-beans.

CUT TO: Wide shot of Sylvia with her brother Roy in the frame.

ROY (WOLF WELP)
How 'bout some coffee?

SYLVIA (PICKPOCKET)
I don't want any coffee. It might put
me to sleep.
(turns back to stirring the beans)

ZOOM IN ON: Beans, bubbling.

PAN TO: Open box of "Argentine Ant Poison"
               on the counter.

PAN BACK TO: Beans, still bubbling.
               (steam rises from them)

V.O.
Who has their paws on the jewels?

Who put the Ant Poison in the pot?

They were just cat's-paws in the
scheme…

The scheme of … *The White Tiger*!

(sloshing & gurgling resume)

Revenge (1918)

When a gal enlists the help
of a man out West to help
find the killer of her fiancé

she ought not to
  select a man who
    has fallen in love with her

but
she
does

& when censors brandish
  their scissors, *they* ought not
    to cut those scenes of tough

dancing nor those
of Tiger Lil shooting
dance hall owner Duncan

but
they
do

and
they
did

As a Young Boy

Here comes an improbably
young Browning, just a kid
Not even eight; negotiating
tickets to his backyard shed

Admission: 5 pins apiece
for the kids lined up –

shuffling like characters
from a *Nancy* strip

Dusty and snotty
pushing each other

March 7, 1887

This date is as precise as the newspaper article in
the *Herald-Post*
of said date
which called Browning:
                            "sprightly"
                                    "bright as a dime"
                                            "a

Barnum, perhaps"

Dramas
        Comedies
                Slapstick
                    Surprise

and tiny wooden figures

washtub-cascade inside

"A Lilliputian aquacade"
chimed in David Skal
(Browning's biographer)

Tiny wooden characters
just a-bobbing in a tub
splashing about to the

squeals of the juvenile audience –
some sort of seagoing disaster –
so much to see for just 5 pins!

And boy
the boy
could sing

Overture: Browning in Blackface

At 12 or 15 Tod Browning
ran away from Kentucky to

step outward
join the circus

developed a crush on one of the dancers which
cooled, but he stayed with the white top world

(Later he'd befriend D.W. Griffith
Settle in Hollywood
Direct sideshow films
like *Freaks* and *Unholy 3*)

Here's a surviving photograph of him
in blackface from the early circus years: [insert
sepia image]

"His eyes meet the viewer's full-on"
reads the caption

Your eyes meet his eyes
&
You search in 'em for regret

Sarcasm
  Trickery
    Vehemence
      Doggerel
        Villainy   *Some*thing in 'em but

all that's there is song and dance
in his glance; his diurnal glance
working cash, makeshift chance

one who barked marks
into shows

& made remarks
through his nose

conducted pickpockets
mastered thaumaturgies

sang some numbers –
some of 'em minstrel shows

some of 'em others
one game or another

because within
those pixelating tents
was everything
in the world

A Young Tod at 15

Then
there was a
beautiful trapeze artist

He fell for her

There's
a pun
in there
some-
where

Circus Jobs

Browning had many

roles – a   Barker a
                  Janitor a
                   Manager a
                   Geek a
                     Conjuror a
                       Conjuror's Assistant a
                         Handcuff Escape Artist a
                       Spieler a
                        Contortionist a
                        and a *Singer*
                        and he'd
                        shamelessly

trace malignancies for the crowds
format the contours of his words

find out what
would please

them whatever would please

them   Anything for 5 pins
            Anything for a buck
              Anything for couple bits

& mostly he excelled as a barker;
luring the marks in –
selling tickets for
sideshows

His intellect = a dowsing rod for coins

Tod's eyes settle on a young man
in a straw hat

passing by
with vacant eyes + a bag of popcorn

Tod's eyes blink
Tod's throat –

It   tunes its pitch:

        "Step this *way*, sir!"

Tod
is making
his mark

Tornado Warning

One time when the circus came into town
after all the tents were set up and billowing
twisters jump-smacked right on top of them

Ka-boom (a detonation)

like an accordion chord
cracking
seemingly
out of nowhere

Maybe it was in a town where the high school
team was the "Centerville Tornadoes" or the
"Doon Cyclones" to give the event some

poetic resonance   or maybe not

The elephants; the tigers – they would have gone
crackers paws mashing spilled popcorn into mud

The clowns would have scurried pell-
mell with their faces ½-way made up;

noses akimbo

The wind whipped   · wild clovers
                        · sawdust
                        · wheel grease
                        · face grease
                        · lace lease
                        · face crease

Here you need to deploy your imagination again
& picture the tent stakes uncorking themselves
from the summer soil up to a blackened sky

Zip – zip – zip – zip

carrying out the directives of the wind
unquestioningly

A disaster which   might occur
had occurred   *was* occurring
                              And wrecking
                              *every*thing

Splintering it   impaling things
Cleaving them open   spraying them
over a crescent-shaped   battlefield

The tent canvas would reach 1,900 feet and
achieve a geocentric orbit for 1 breath
before it billowed back to earth and
shrouded itself; settling itself
over dimpled-circus-ruin

Dinner for 2 at 8

Tod Browning once said of Chaney, "There
wasn't a thing he wouldn't turn his hand to"

Lon Chaney returned the compliment
They were like sea lions
at each other

After a steak dinner sitting across
a table-clothed plane
from each other
in a darkened
Hollywood
restaurant

Chaney was snuffing-out half-smoked
cigarettes in grisly gristle even before
the waiter had offered them lick-mints

Browning would have had quite a few
since he invariably had had quite a few
Mr. Browning was soaked in his spirits

Chaney was stone sober not because he
was the more disciplined of the pair –
Either of them had enough discipline

To choke a horse
Discipline was not

what they lacked   Discipline
                                     they had

a-plenty

What they might have done
with a little more of
was even a modicum
of mutual affection

After their 10th film they hunched forward
like they had both gotten inside &
were about to land successive
blows-to-the-body; yet they
seethed with respect for
each other

Each

stared at each other like they were waiting for the
ref to finish his admonishments –

> *I want a nice clean fight, you*
> *2*

> *& protect yourselves at all*
> *times*

On the set of *Mark of the Vampire* (1935)

FADE IN:

INT. MOVIE STUDIO SET – DAY
Sights and sounds of crew members scurrying about
and cast members rehearsing their lines.

                    MS. BORLAND
          How about if I hiss? – Like an angry
          cat?

                    MR. BROWNING
          (surprised)
          Try it.

                    MS. BORLAND
          (hissing dramatically)

CAMERA MOVES IN ON BROWNING'S FACE

                    MR. BROWNING
          Print it.

                                        CUT TO:

INT. MOVIE SET -- NIGHT

                    MS. BORLAND
          (grimacing as she navigates a stairwell)

                    MR. BROWNING
          Cut and print. That's a wrap.

We see crew scrambling for the next scene.

                    MR. BROWNING (CONT.)
          (turns to Borland, hands on his clipboard)
          You gave me something with your mouth.

                         MS. BORLAND
          I twisted my ankle.

                        MR. BROWNING
          (maintaining eye contact)
          Try twisting it again.

The Depression

In *Dracula* (1931) –
the image of the bat
and the stagecoach

(flapping &
just hovering
above the seat
where the driver
was supposed to have been
just as empty as a stomach)

mirrored how many folks
felt about their navigators
during those tough-grey-years

The stagecoach – they had just
assumed – was in capable hands
or at least some manner of hands

while in fact the wheels were tugged
(like an old magnet collecting filings)
by the *flap-flap-flap* of a bat flapping

to a mossed-over castle
populated with vamps
cored out from trolls

bat guano in columns
dim rot poured from
a corkscrewed hole

a lichen-thick castle

whose stones shifted
at any demon's scold

which sure was not where
they'd hoped to be going

An Unmade Movie with Johnny Eck

Johnny Eck – the charismatic actor
who disappeared below-the-chest –

ambulated on his arms with the
grace and confidence of a skater

Magnetically affable and captivating
he stole the stage in *Freaks* (1932)

Another film was soon in the works
as Eck's autobiography relates:

> Browning was working on a script
> concerning more body modification
>
> A mad scientist assembling
> criminals from body parts
>
> A starry vehicle for Johnny Eck 'the half-
> boy' & his 'normal' identical-twin Robert
>
> Inspired by the Eck twins' days
> together in vaudeville in which

>> Robert planted himself in the
>> audience playing the role of a stooge
>> volunteer
>>
>> for a magician's sawing-in-half trick
>> from which would emerge two
>> halves

1: a midget hidden in an oversize
pants

2: Johnny himself gaily skipping
about to horrified caterwauls of the
audience so full & gratified with
their just tickets

Another Unmade Movie (1933)

After *Fast Workers* lost twice as
much for MGM than *Freaks* Tod

was paired with Wm. Faulkner & went
into the swamp outside New Orleans

In the steaming shrimp camps
Faulkner – before he was fired –

before Tod was fired
and the script scuttled –

related a platform constructed
in the water with sheds upon it

a platform where Faulkner was admonished
to "forget the story and just write dialogue"

A platform

> "with a single wall on it, so that when
> you opened the door and stepped
> through it, you stepped right off into
> the ocean itself. As they built it, on the
> first day, the Cajun fisherman
> paddled up in his narrow tricky
> pirogue made out of a hollow log. He
> would sit in it all day long in the
> broiling sun watching the strange
> white folks building this strange
> imitation platform. The next day he

was back in the pirogue with his
whole family, his wife nursing the
baby, the other children, and the
mother-in-law, all to sit all that day in
the broiling sun to watch this foolish
and incomprehensible activity"

without even having to
buy tickets to see it
Faulkner recalled
years later
glumly

Uncharged Vehicular Manslaughter (1915)

Four years before Tod Browning met Lon Chaney
& they toiled through 10 films, Browning crashed:

Early headlights cut through none of the darkness so
in those days, a passenger would step out of the car
& illuminate a path with a torchlight on foot, pacing

safely & softly *weave*-wafting around hazards
punctuating the rainy darkness
zig-zagging between obstacles

zip-zip-zip

None of that one night of drinking & driving back
from a tavern;

Browning's carelessness sheared doilies of gore; a
crescent bitten

abruptly   Ka-*boom* (a detonation again)
                & seemingly out of nowhere –

Deftly adhering to Newton's 3rd Law of Motion –
steel bars from a railroad flatbed pierced
the car's windshield & the passenger's face

The Los Angeles Times' report
was as grotesque as a Browning film:

> "The impresses in his skull were as
> even & regular as the design of a
> waffle off the grill."

The impresses in the skull
did not belong there

The skull had belonged to
comedic actor Elmer Booth

He'd starred in *Musketeers of Pig Alley*
with Lilian Gish three years earlier

Now there was a Rorschach Test
all over the street composed of wet
bits of Booth & Browning –
but mostly of Booth

The bits of Browning
were all of his teeth

& thereafter Browning always
wore a moustache to cover the
damaged mandibles; to provide
a hairy-haven for the scaring; a
sheltered effigy of curved mutilation

Browning's left leg was mangled
requiring months in a cauldron
Afterwards he walked with a limp

Some critics self-revealingly speculate
an unplugging; that that night
Browning also suffered
some serious unnamed
injury to his genitals,

explaining the
recurring
images of
castration
in his films

There's no evidence

  of such an injury

So this is really hitting

  below the belt

   [insert cymbal crash]

London After Midnight (1927)

London After Midnight – a lost Browning/Chaney
"masterpiece" which we're allowed to claim –

lacking much evidence to either confirm or rebut
the assertion

other than the recollections of surviving viewers

           such as Robert Bloch who
           stopped surviving in 1994

Lon Chaney at his most horrible
the top hat, facial skin stretched

        taut
          which
            taught
             a
               potent
                oedipal
                  contamination

The ghastly, dusty hair dyed with dread
flowery decay atop that strong skullcap

Those terrible teeth
too many of them

An improbable
gleaming set
of bite mitcs

ticking…

It's the cut-scenes from this lost-film which
steam in rambunctious mists. Let's consider:

1.   Sir James having trouble telling Lucy the
        grim truth

        The remaining stills themselves seem to
        drag

2.   Burke (back in London and) giving his
        theory of hypnotism a work-out on a busy
        street

3.   A trio emerging from a nighttime brush
        The camera is stationary. Fade in.
        One carries a rifle. One an axe.

        The third – the tallest – with a white neck
        scarf and a lantern

        Lighting the moss from the trees
        Stop. Startled. A lifeless figure
        Lies crumpled.

4.   Harry was found dead.

        "Two …
                    little …
                              marks –
        Here!"

The cut-scenes from a lost-film
Doublets of what's gone missing

Two little marks
which are not
here
at all

2 little lost marks

but
still

it's the
"Harry's been found –
dead"

that
cannot
be un-marked

nor
un-wrapped

Silk Stocking Sal (1924)

When Tod Browning's
Silk Stocking Sal opened
at the Grand Ordway in one
small town or another in August
1924 the preposterous crowds adored it

The film itself

> like most of the *Film
> Booking Offices of America*
> films starring Ms. Evelyn Brent

is lost

Wiped away

Though certainly a few
silver nitrate crumbles of it
exist in landfills – pressed

under layer
upon layer
of detritus –

softly demolished
evenly sandwiched
with fragments of egg
and soggy torn overalls
stained with tractor drippings

In *Sal*, John Gough was cast as the 'Gopher'

Alice Wilson played 'Bargain Basement' Annie

Evelyn herself was
'Stormy' Martin herself

Was no one 'Sal'?

and whatever *became*
of her silk stockings?

Chaney's Face

Chaney's visage was its most cadaverous not when playing the kelpie but the villain. His visage was troubling. Scowling. Not icy but warm, strong, and misguided. Sweaty. Gracefully scheming and taut. Braided with a brand of twine that might be inked with a cursive script across the shipment crates in the hold which contain heavy scrolls of it: "Retribution."

Those butterfly eyebrows set to skewer his peepers. Again, the teeth – unnaturally perfect. The tension between wanting to look away and holding his grimace. An oscillating plasticity. A mischievous hostility.

In this way, his face pays its regards to cadavers.

Chaney's face does not radiate the warmth of warm. It radiates something practiced of a blank etiology. It wraps itself around and around and around you – which is not something an ordinary man or woman fancies when it comes to cadavers.

The Unknown (1927) · I

Browning loved
circling the circus

repeatedly
fashioning

it into gothic
melodramas

for profit
this time:

How does the armless knife-thrower
the fake-freak Alonzo not impale

        the one he loves –
        the circus owner's daughter?

Whose arms will encircle
the demimonde –

This vixen –   Nanon
         The daughter of Zanzi?

         with her anxiety of men's arms
         which paw at her like hooves

Whose double-thumb will leave
tell-tale prints of the murder?

Why Alonzo's, of course

His double-thumb will
do the telling

unless he
silences it –
trouble-chum –

     -   the circus and
     -   his double-thumb

& then-some …

The Unknown (1927) · II

The florid crimson movie poster
posed as a barker for the marks

& the marks bought tickets in piles
as if they were fetish-salad-sundaes

piles of them
tied between horses
trammeling opposed treadmills
forced to rip off the arms of a rival until
hooved in the chest into a kind of stage mush

Such a stampede of red-profits
set off by a stampede-of-ripping!

Such are
the marks

Now we'll ask –
as the film requires:

From whence

does deformity derive? For
Alonzo does disarm himself

His arms are removed
by a blackmailed doc

spoilation of the double-thumb
yes, but more to make

himself lovely
to his Nanon

only to be rejected
by the armed miss

& miss his arms

Rather 'disarming'
one might even say

I did say ('disarming')

Thus, only as an armless
ersatz could Alonzo woo

Thus, the genuineness of
deformity plays its part

of which
an arm

is a part both
before & after

it's been parted
from his flesh

"I've lost a little" (flesh)
Alonzo once concedes

to Nanon sheepishly
and that part was

genuine justice the
justice of a circus

& here's a motif
in that vein
from the veins: Opposed horses will
                    play executioners
                    (which they do

     because
     at the
     scrunched beating center
     of *The Unknown*
     – a 'psychosexual grotesquerie'
          some say –

     trembles the anxiety of
     fetid extremities-castration)

You know

what they say – 'You can find
                    anything at the circus'

But it's unclear what we'd find
between Browning's own legs
according to a blouse-huck of
squirming deviant circus-critics

of
a
certain

bent

writing
in a
cement
tent

with a
tangy
scent

that
they
spent

to
pay
the
rent
&

whom
we
might
justi-
fiably
call

bent

The Unknown (1927) · III

Step right up, folks, for a tire-tread-worn tale of:

Boy meets Girl
Boy loves Girl

2nd seemingly-armless   Boy loves Girl too

& has the initial advantage, being seemingly arm-
less since Girl suffers from an 'appendage phobia'

then to 'seal the deal'
as they say (& i said)

Boy 2 *un*arms himself
(surgically-speaking)

Meanwhile   Girl (now) loves
arms!

Girl (now) loves
Boy 1

having recovered from her phobia overnight
and fallen into the open arms of a strongman

(Boy 1)

while Boy 2 recovers from his surgery in bed

&   upon realizing
with al-arm
the new state
of affairs

Boy 2 regrets
his 'farewell
to arms'

having relinquished
his right to bear-arms
via his act of self-
harm

&   so sets out to
remove both-arms

(they were no
'brothers
in arms')

of
Boy 1

Browning @ Church

Enter:

Columned oppressors of Enoch

Tyrants in coalition with the pejorative
Who thrust pruninghook spears rudely
Who will mingle infants with the asp
I'll call them: *Maher-shalal-hash-baz*
Cast them: Haste spoil – speed booty
Arranging six cockatrice tears toward
Seven soft-winged manlike creatures
Whisking snail eggs perversely laid
The worst lack all but a conviction
While they themselves they stew it

All this venom is mere autonomy
Taunting any cock's comb crown
With "Little king, little king, what
Do you do?" tan-chorus-matted to
Jerusalem's threshing-room floor
(straw trodden down the dunghill)
Bel boweth down, Nebo stoopeth
Vomit-spill Sennacherib's tribute
Upon the eager night hags before
Sawing a Deutero-Isaiah asunder

Exit:

Apocalypse of an exile to be

The Virgin of Stamboul (1920)

Priscilla Dean plays the part
of the Muslim beggar Sari
as if she were some gum-
smacking Jersey tomboy

This worn love triangle plot –
wherein the American officer
wins the girl from the Sheik –
is riven through with prayer

     Sari's prayers
     Whisperings

     Lit from above
     Angled to God

     To slip between
     Rafters and ascend

     like notes from
     a church organ

     or incense from
     a withered puck

     Some gates open
     only on the inside

The souq fills with birds
alighting on Sari's smile
& everywhere like snow

flakes spliced betwixt
silhouettes of cavalry,
the desert sands, and
wide-striped costumes

Overhearing a rumor
that her soul is as
"dirty as the streets"

she cobblestone-tiptoes
into a mosque for prayer
despite the title cards'
assertions of some-

thing "cruel and truly
oriental" embroidered
in Islam: "women,"

the producers claimed,
"have no souls" with
a cruelty of their own –

the producers' own –
which they now own

Soiled-Round Solid-Bound Roots

Browning grew up in Louisville
  (which is firmly in the South
  according to Kentuckians
  and not even *close* to the South
  according to South Carolinians

  who think that the Mason-Dixon
  line was drawn by Northerners
  & that the farthest North you can go
  before you're not South anymore
  is in the upper reach of Georgia)

Browning left with the circus &
     he never looked back
     never came back
     not even for a parent's funeral

After a while the circus turned into Hollywood
but it was all the same vaudeville big top to him

The soil of the place
  would never completely
  wash out of his pants

While he was still in the real circus
He would have returned periodically
To Louisville's home-cooked meals
When the circus came (back) to town

There's a scrap in the back of a magician's trade
publication that just might be Houdini looking for
Tod's whereabouts

In those circus days
we can't be sure
but regard-less

we can be sure
of the soil
he took with him
all the way
home

Intermission: Browning's Journal

In the freshness of 11:00
It seemed absolutely clear
To me that they had spent
Their collective mornings
At the Pollack Circus nearby

They smelled like popcorn
… I guess that's why
Although the circus is not
The only place to buy the
Manna of the make-believe

I observed them and wrote
Surreptitiously, I figured,
While sipping my poison
In a place I wish wasn't
'Jim's Coffee' but was

Actually my former lover's
Gin-joint financed with
A loan from me never repaid
And only mentioned once when
She told me to 'act like an adult'

Moreover, there are other items
Mothers & daughters buy there
That these 2 hadn't – such as
painted hippos, toy llamas,
Stuffed anteasters, and the like and

Actually, stuffed anteasers haven't
Been available at circus shops

Except at Pollacks' for 25 years
So that would have been a dead
Giveaway except that it wasn't

A dead giveaway because a dead
Giveaway would emit a mightier
Reek than stale popcorn any day
Of the week. And at that moment
They both turned their eyes on me,

Marched right over to where I sat
Spat backwards, clicked their wrists,
Recited the 3rd verse of *How Great
Thou Art*, and smiled fakely. Then
They winked

    Ta-da

and became popcorn

Fast Workers (1933)

A tale of two riveters
Gunner and Bucker
Pals true and staunch

Enter now Mary
What a tough dame
Slapstick tricks a plenty

But Act 3 is just another
horror film 4-shadowed

By the ballet of rivets
which go just like this –

>1. Battered in heat, red-hot in a three-legged
>gnathobase
>
>2. Plucked out with tongs
>
>3. Arm swing one, two, three, away!
>
>4. An ellipse-tip steel-hovering, & into the
>riveter's catch
>
>5. Then out of that & into the beam: *rat-a-tat-tat-that-tat*!

All dizzy-diagonally 65-stories up
Open steel scaffolding for security

2x8 lumber akimbo for footholds

which a vengeful foot dislodges

and silently nosedives out of frame
Gunner next pitches inside the frame

He's in an unsustainable pose
one amphetamine rivet lets go

      · Then two

      · Then three

Gunner's sweater stretches… snaps
Discretely releasing him into opening
See his cropper plummet end-over-end

Keyboard Accompaniment

No one could covet the fetters therein

Imprisoned for life in factory walls

Italians, Greeks, Irish, and Bedouins

Toiling for pay, stretching wire, fingers raw
Young, they just fabricated what they saw

He'd just turned northwest on North Vermont Street
Lost (but carefree) with no one Tod could call

A tall mast in the fog troubled his feet
The last person he'd expected to meet

Stilled in his throat a horse *vox humana*

As it ribbed in his mind scenes far from sweet

That bricked-in place where they craft pianos

    Los Feliz's grease-
    pail olfactory

    pause-haltered him
    The rag-time factory

Pre-Browning or Unlike a Vaudeville Organ

Setting:

Five days' walk from Paris (1680)

Props:

· Virtue-dreams formed in a daffodil
· Loose wool
· Chipped ivory

Characters:

· François Couperin (age 12)
· A new organ at L'eglise Notre Dame

Premise:

Everything is a handiwork

So, he skipped there
the leaves whispering under
the calfskin soles of his shoes

He fell upon the ravishingly naive
instrument as a kind of a greeting
His skin was pink. Hers was maple.

The boy's pinkie teased the lower G
the walls buzzed and versicles chimed

Tibbles notes "a luminous dialogue between

grand orgue and the *positi*." No arguments

The organ's articulations stilled all gossip
It incubated God-speech pipes of metallic
novelty-harvests a thousand miles distant

Tibbles again gushed of the instrument:
"The flamboyance of the *voix humaine*"
Even its deficiencies radiated an "instab-
ility of winding and tuning an uneven-
ness or slowing pipe speech" unstopped

The notes in the
upper register seem
to have been beveled
wordlessly within
tight angles created
by the church nave

And those notes feel
beveled within one's
body as they sound

In Couperin's first mass
the Kyrie *fugue* derived
from a chant incipit

His harmonic idioms
called upon things
rather insistently

More, they thumped
with recognition

they sang of adhesion

Stillness intersected with flight
and bisected the human heart
hewing open to receive feathers

Couperin was so young
So was the new organ

Neither were slit
off from anything

Both were childish
in the very best sense

Name Change

At some unspecified age – and
for some unspecified reason
Charles Albert Browning
changed his name to
Tod which – in
German –
means
death

The Big City (1928)

Slyly, in *The Big City*, Tod
cast an actor named Virginia
to play a lady named Tennessee
but whose actual name is Texas

    It may seem improbable
    that anyone could lose *The*
    Big City but that is what
    has happened (or nearly so)

    The last known print was
    mailed to Australia in 1950 –
    then returned – then burned
    in the great vault fire of '65

    An electrical short in MGM's
    Vault 7 in the backlot set spark
    to so many cans of silver nitrate
    the initial explosion killed a man

    The concrete bunk houses were
    impervious to thieves but not
    to fire lacking sprinklers
    and just one small bony fan

    Nitrate film can spontaneously
    combust at only 106° F and
    wound film burns underwater so
    sprinklers may have done no good

F. Gwynplaine MacIntyre claims

to have encountered an unnamed
gentleman in Europe who held
eight old cannisters of partially

deteriorated film marked *Le loup de
soie noire* (The Wolf of Black Silk)
which was, in fact, *The Big City* –
an unauthorized bicycle print of it

in the late 1990s and viewed it
on a handheld Steenbeck viewer
But Gwynplaine later died when
he set fire to his own collection

Man & Woman Perform Foxtrot w/o Heads

In the 3rd reel, Tennessee introduces
the 'Headless Dancers' act which is
just that, the film having revealed
that the illusion is achieved by black
velvet (or perhaps silk in the French
version) hoods over a black background
by which they appear to be headless

But Red previously abducted the real
fake dancers and replaced them with
imposter fake dancers who brandish
revolvers and rob the stunned audience
winking at Red Watson as they snatch
his cufflinks; suggesting Red's guilt

Next at the hideout Red waits for the
loot when the real imposter dancers
break through (gagged) from the closet
to his chagrin and realization that he
has been double-crossed by the Arab

The Show (1927) · I

A play within a play
Illusions within illusions
A show within 'the show'

Ballyhoo man Cock Robin
draws the curtain to reveal:

    1st: The ticket-taker: The Living Hand of
    Cleopatra

    Next: Zela the Half-Lady

    3rd: Arachnida the Human Spider
    rose bud lips centered in her web –
    A neck with nothing below it

    4th: Neptuna the Mermaid
    All scales from torso down

Their common denominator:
Truncation of the lower body

Then 5th our Cock Robin
disappears to re-costume
as John-the-Baptist who
meets Salome's gambit

    his beard conveniently
    obscures where a head
    may or may not
    have separated

from shoulders
and plots a path
into a basket –
(another truncation)

while

somewhere offstage
a tea kettle screams

all of this simmering
in the oils of reptiles

for as all we'll soon see
an iguana lurks in the attic

The Redemption Arc:

First: Cock Robin – the grifter
separating rich sheep herder
daughters from their riches

    without remorse
    with sleigh-of-hand
    a confidence game

    Blessed with dark flashing eyes
    Ladies cannot resist his charms

Then: twitching with a goodness
      scheming eyes cannot avert
      cemented to the camera

    · Unblinking
    · Astounded
    · Penetrating

The longest unbroken stare in the history of
cinema

Until it breaks him and his wickedness in twain
and

It separates rancid-soup-onions and toxins from
him

What once we saw (behind-the-stage) as
machines

Dimly now we see revealed behind dark eyes
An uncovering being repaired slightly

Nine years later the gorgeous John Gilbert died
Re-stewed in a barrel of gin – but before then
Marlene Dietrich could not resist him

Nor Garbo herself
although later she
was a no-show at
their wedding

Wicked Darling (1919)

Amongst Paula Dean's
magnificent twitching eyebrows
seared weeds flourished
with 2 soiled petals
tossed back in
the gutter: *Splash*

                         splash!

'Rose Mary' – she'd slip him the icy mitt
'cause (she thought) he'd lost all his kale

which
he had – but
the kale which mattered
weren't dough – she was
more than square
and good she

was wonderful   as the pearls she hid beneath
                         the dirt
                         of her houseplant
                         'though *she'd* been

tossed
quick
in
the gutter

herself by 'Stoop Connors' more than once
& *he'd* had the crap *kicked* out of him thrice:

Kick

        kick

kick

What the audience ought not to lose sight of weren't
trenchant pearls beneath a soaked-peat-in-a-pot-of-it

but rather a
kale of a
different
class of
the cat's
pajamas

that
Paula
Dean
wore

Outside the Law (1920)

"Catch this Woman she's out-
side the Law," read the ads

Out from poppy perfumed conduits rose
the crest of a yellow torrent wherein a
braying betrayed a kind of prophecy

Paula Dean could recite six chapters of
The Iliad with her eyes in half-a-reel &
in the frames of Tod Browning's she did

Chinatown glowed in the darkness like
a duel; dancing headlights right-on-cue

The claustrophobia of jewel thieves in a
hideout with a kid's arms round 2 necks

Dapper Bill's vomit-hued paisley tie tugs
on an arc of a stray bullet or 2 & the sun-

dial of a lawman's badge across the hall
where a cat brings all her kittens to nurse

That was that which Black Mike had overlooked
Bang! Silky Mol had protection lessons readied

That which Black Mike had overlooked was
the human heart trained for circus-aim justice

He had practically tripped over it
not as if it had been planted there

A Lost Film That Reads Like a Gorgon

Anguished sensibilities & trauma comprise most
films joyous, achievement, holiness, romance, pals
'n grit take a plaid-backseat to unrequited love &
gnashing

Poetry blanks with the dying of the sight & a cob-
roller slouching tards Bethlehem Steel– not-with a
transient breeze; lemon popcorn nor morning papers
on th' bed

Anorexia sells better than earned contentment
A Singapore sling spells better-than-lemonade
Dementia outdoes childhood – ten or eleven:1

Think 6 tin-glasses of lemonade were vulgar – but
Concoct coconut flies in 'em & unawares maidens
About to drink-it-down runnel – tap *that* lyricism:

    Like maple from back-in-Tennessee shelter
    Belts busted-up under chins from which it
    Drips and drips and drips and runs away

    Luckless men untimely ripped from wagons
    Picking at things that don't need pickings-at
    The stink of bad flesh; the Lord taketh away

    Warm spit left o're from loved ones' epileptic
    fittings cataloging a genocide with the dewey
    decimal system spilled-spit lit-propane on 2
    children who merited not

Sawing coffins in coldest spatter
3 legs torn off in a mangled mess
Their diaries tatter-puss & gone a

A crusty sideburn, a crackling somethin'
Starts the clatterin' of an engine floodin'

Whoosh

    Whoosh

        Whoosh

    Hurt residin' deeper than one has ta-hurt

That slouching beast: leave a' well enough alone
But inside this geode-sickness is the sourest milk
Clay-pot-horses gone mad wiff sunken rat-teeth

Tod's film too, in making its point, bunts 1/2-
indecisively but it wraps up with a brass band &
sunshine expandin'

Not with something's demise; some bard's banner
o' rot

Tickets-for-sale
Tickets-for-sale

Freaks (1932)

Enter not the not-something
to be grasped nor emptying
to take the form-of-a-slave
but the filling out of ego:
Beastliness and mastery

Wither in this anti-kenosis
the freaks did have a law a
law-written on-their-hearts
They chanted their rules
They cooked Cleo in them

     We accept her
     We accept her

     One of us
     One of us

     Gobble-gobble
     Gobble-gobble

so when she emerged as a sort
of cooked goose ready for the
market and the accumulation of
peona damni buffalo nickels
to be exchanged 4 somethings

A snaking of elephants fitted
with amputation construction –
a *guignolesque* apotheosis –
A circus-justice of undoing
staged for the ticker-holders

"'barker' is never used in a carnival"

Sword-Swallower
Mannix takes
over here 4 me:

"Bally, everybody!"

Enter: A horse-faced thin-man
Ragged cuffs scissor-trimmed

& the swallower
further relates:

Draw the tip
with fire

Tod learned
the first night
'tip' meant crowd

& to

light the torches
to draw the tip

Soak the heads in the gas
Produce a pot-bellied flute
Make it wail
as if its tail
is kicked out of him *kick*

kick

kick

From the platform imagine what Tod could see:
A forest of bespangled tents & sparkling lights

   Well above the head of the crowd
   The crowd's head
   Forests glimmering and the eyes

    Chants of gamblers
      Dances of the midway
        Shouts of the talkers
         Music from 3
          bands

Spokes of the Ferris wheel

It's the turning of the tip wherein blisters are made
It's in the turning of the tip where change is made

whole

Touch his finger; bless the *djinni*
So much to see for just five pins

Film Editing: An Apology

The thickened door crept open on its hinge
Crisp whiffs of dirty cotton accumulated
Along the step, extolling motionlessness

An unexceptional observation
In terms such-as-these; visually –
Yet the deviations prove a ruling

A more discursive examination might reveal
Something tangy and stringy and wet moving
Within, shifting its weight in our green guts

Like the lyrics to Blind Willie Johnson's "Dark
was the Night" spread over a layer of neurons

The smooth
 plastered interior
 of a lighthouse

It is in these caverns
 where discernment shifts
 and it *is* wet
  this turning inward
   this emotive implosion
    'Tis the mark of a tick-tock
    frame-by-frame de-acceleration

 Thus:

He speaks - he moves; even thinks

84

The viewer sees the interior shot
Pistols are fired at him & his pals

So internally, he's inverse to his external
rapidity

He's patiently thoughtful. Methodical.
Effective.

Meanwhile, this crusty door still inches
Toward opening, commencing: *Creak*

Where East is East (1929)

And where exactly *is* East
East?

one might
ask
as i did

Well, Laos

in which
it's the familiar
ballyhoo story of

    · Boy meets Girl

    · Boy loves Girl

    · Boy meets
    Girl's Mother –

    and loves *her* too

        which (predictably) angers
        Girl's Father

        so –
        (predictably)

    · Girl's Father
releases
Gorilla

· Gorilla
mains Girl's Father

· Gorilla
kills Girl's Mother

· Boy marries Girl

· Both flee Laos

to escape this
kind of craziness

Kultur des Todes

The sack of shoats tied to the calcified stone
Of her heart and thrown into the river of his
Damaged psyche, his being, his wasted thoughts.
They were thus clad in a shameful human parody.

A burgundy fish monger, an isolated love.
This dear. She stood above the porcelain cavity.
Firmly fixed in this geography: a dismal vessel.
A domed sty; urban pocket; dreadful row.

The character retrieves the shoats, smearing the
Pink noses with the precision of an office machine;
Predictability of a narcotic-notorious principally
For its smooth surfaces, stacks; stacks of sameness.

Tightly framed by the wall's tiny ceramic piazzas
The burlap square now filled its vision like a field
Rushing towards a parachute-less diver, his back
To the sky we stared at after she had left the square.

Primeval monotonous-ness is her coadjutor,
Bearing allegiance as a prisoner to daylight.
A bucketful of dead owls. Take commission of it.
Acquitted of reason, dull devotee of formalism.

The emptiness invokes an undulating optimism
Festooned with a kind of bias, not for its vexed
Possibilities, or its promises, but for its vacancy,
While in the other room, we can hear them mewing.

Through the door, I could hear them mewing.

Such oblivion is as magnanimous as it is grateful.
It coats the surface of the burlap sack - and the tile
Into which we propel, headlong, sucking inward.

Such rottenness is what's expected from 'poets' –
Petty. Pretty only in their vacuity; their self-
made-ness; and while delivered here in spades
They'll have no part of it. 'Tis not an agency.

Another Lost Browning Film

Crouching behind a blooming blue deed
Wrapped in outdoor branches splayed
Across the un-tended library shelf
Clown #1 fidgets while un-intended

He waits -   Un-pretended
His warts -   Un-distended

Whispering a worthless collapsed sigil
Scratching it into the *Lumière Domitor*
Praying some torch-demon unearth them

(Her teachers would have commented
On the grotesque waste for such aims –
Or how to *shore up* effects of a past sin
With such operationally dim musculature

That is: Not very effectively)

Before: Steaming dumplings on the dumbwaiter
            had arrived into this

But a stiff wind through the broken window
            quashed their appeal

Then: A great deal of re-setting

They had not bread nor
Life for that time-being

She'd found no prince, nor price

But for these
clowns

He'd complain, all right
But with un-ease

Until they all fell through a pre-constructed escape
hatch

Lensing in cooling grace of a sort
And he stiffened as she stretched
Providentially for the old camera

With their interiors de-marked
               & innards cleaned
                  ready for the show

West of Zanzibar (1928)

Anna leaves Phroso 4 Crane
Crane cripples Phroso –
Phroso becomes 'Dead Legs'

18 months later Anna returns
with a beautiful blonde baby
Maizie (just learning to walk)

Cuckolded 'Dead Legs' crawls into the cathedral

confronting 3 icons:
        · Saint Joseph in stained glass
        · Madonna and
        · Infant in stone

Beneath them 3 beings:

        · 'Dead Legs' crawling
        · Maizie (the crying infant)
        · The beautiful Anna, dead

Both sets of 3 framed
within the cloistral place

With inversion, 'Dead Legs' swears an oath to the
Madonna to exact revenge on the adulterous Crane
and his brat-child and 'Dead Legs' burrows into the
darkest law-columned vat

18 years pass…   'Dead Legs' dispatches
                        Crane

whereupon true parenthood is
revealed

'Dead Legs' reconfigured: as 'Daddy
Long Legs'

From which emerges this Hollywood priesthood:

· Teenaged Maize as Madonna with
cornstalk-silk hair
· A 'Dead Legs' Dad crucified offscreen

Beneath which remain 3 beings
Framed outside the frames
Framed of the *fuga mundi*

That's *West of Zanzibar*
4 u

Tod Browning's Estate Plan

Tod's property emulsified
behind his very eyes with
the realization that all his
wiccan nitrate spell royalties

might be
trickier
to devise

than he'd
originally
anticipated

Non-probate avenues to consider;
Angles to take stock of; The
right wording of the thing

Should the gift be conditioned –
Will the devisee accept it some
time after the donor is cremated –

Ought he
to die
intestate –

Will other expectancies be
roiled / calamitous
soiled / cantankerous?

What of *lapse*; of loved
ones who refused to die
in the correct sequence?

How about *abatement*; of
creditors consuming legacies
as if they were candy corn?

problematic-postmortem-presents,
these

The ink on the testator's papers was
still wet when he realized his mistake

The Armstrong-Schroder, Beverly Hills

Skal tell us how

> "Thirty-one Malibu Colony became a
> solitary fortress for Browning in the
> postwar years, its porch guarded by
> an impassive bronze statue of a
> fisherman, frozen in the act of peering
> at the ocean. The world rarely
> intruded, and usually only at
> Browning's invitation. But there were
> occasional surprises."

Yet Tod skipped
Bela Lugosi's funeral
in August of 1956

& that wasn't a surprise

Dr. Snow would take Tod to lunch
at the Armstrong-Schroeder
on Wilshire and Spalding
to meet old cronies

who sadly began to die off;
few others recognized Tod
anymore but when they did

he would just beam
like a lightning bug
at the surprise of it

A Malibu neighbor
of Browning's did
marry Lugosi's
4th wife
in 1966
but

Tod skipped that too
He was dead by then
So, no surprise there

Have you tried our special
de-luxe hamburger steak

Roast young
tom turkey savory dressing

Italian spaghetti
our special meat sauce

Scrambled calf's
brains and eggs

Half an avocado
with mixed fruit

Special made
knack-wurst

Mexican tamale
homemade chili

Creamed turkey
a la king (served on a
patty shell)

Have you tried our
little-thin hot-cakes

Have you tried our special
de-luxe hamburger steak
with or without onions

Finis: End-of-Life

Browning had run off to the circus as a boy
and you can take the boy out of Louisville
but you can't take the Louisville
out of the boy
they say
I say…

All his life, Tod smoked a now-forgotten brand of
Louisville cigarettes

A recluse, he drank a case of Coors a day and
smoked & in the end, the Clowns killed him;
Clowns – the Louisville cigarette which Tod
smoked –

As a doctor extracted Tod's larynx in June of 1962;
Browning re-entered the silent era then he had a
succession of strokes (here we imagine the sounds
of a succession of strokes…)

PARTIAL DARKNESS:

PAN TO:

MR. BROWNING
(writing)

P.O.V. behind his back; we can see him clutching a
pen and paper. As his pen flows, on the page
appears:

FIRE IS HOT

FIRE IS HOT
 FIRE IS HOT
  FIRE IS HOT
   FIRE IS HOT

                    V.O.
Was Tod scratching out his own title
cards –

Was his heart latticed by the circus
as a boy?

Or pickled by Coors as a grown
clown?

On the day he died … had he
touched upon *Timor Gehennalis*?

The scheme of … *Timor
Gehennalis*?

                    BRIGHT DAYLIGHT:

FADE TO: EXT. BROWNING'S HOUSE

There was no funeral. Browning insisted.

Title card

[Finis]

Two Endnotes of Note

i.

Like World War I – which drew itself
to a close 10 years before the end of
the silent era – no one then called it
'one' and no one called them
'silent' and no one called
them 'black and white'
either

ii.

Browning's right hand:
His fingers would have
reckoned a certain way

If you ever shook hands with him
his hand would be firm or brittle
distracted or indecisive
Perhaps simply vague
A little moist more
likely intelligent
caring of craft
meticulous
precise
sad

but I've done some scouring &
no recollections exist-in-print
and soon the last people who
ever juddered his hand will
themselves yen without

having recorded it and
that 2 will be swabbed
away like burning
film in a concrete
circus-justice
catacomb
vault
gone
end

Turpentine Lumber in 8 Stanzas

The timber of most poetry today
partakes of Tod Browning films

Crippled, rent, and soused
in an entertainment-ether of

Amputations & bi-transformations
Drowsing-rod oak-specie nihilism

A nadir of self-becoming
Some-kind of carnival it's

A dim distraction
in full-swing its

Refreshments
in participles

but lacking
an artifact

It lacks
popcorn

[cymbal crash]

ACKNOWLEDGEMENTS

Browning in Blackface was published by NINE MUSES POETRY (Dec. 2019)

Tornado Warning, Uncharged Vehicular Manslaughter (1915) and *Chaney's Face* were published by THIRTEEN MINA BIRDS (Aug. 2020)

A slightly different version of *Tod Browning's Estate Plan* was published as *Estate Planning* in SCARLET LEAF REVIEW (Nov. 2020)

Louisville Herald Post, March 7, 1887

Los Angeles Times, June 16, 1915

Time, July 24, 1936

Martin F. Norden and Madeleine A. Cahill, "Violence, Women, and Disability in Tod Browning's *Freaks* and *The Devil-Doll*: The Shows of Violence," 26 *The Journal of Popular Film and Television* (Spring 1998) 86.

David Pierce, "The Legion of the Condemned – Why American Silent Films Perished," 9 *Film History* 5 (1997)

"Johnny Eck," in *Pandemonium: Freaks, Magicians, & Movie Stars* issue 3 (Cambridge: Living Color Productions, 1989)

Michael F. Blake, *A Thousand Faces: Lon Chaney's Unique Artistry in Motion Pictures* (Vestal, NY: Vestal Press, 1997)

"William Faulkner," in Malcolm Cowley, ed., *Writers at Work: The Paris Review Interviews* (New York: Viking Press, 1958)

Gilles Deleuze, *Cinema I: The Movement Image* (Hugh Tomilson and B. Habberjam, trans.) (Minneapolis, MN: University of Minnesota Press, 1986)

Bernd Herzogenrath, ed., *The Cinema of Tod Browning: Essays of the Macabre and Grotesque* (Jefferson, NC: McFarland & Company, Publishers, 2008)

Bernd Herzogenrath, ed., *The Films of Tod Browning* (London: Black Dog Publishing, 2006)

Daniel P. Mannix, *Freaks: We Who Are Not Others* (New York: Pocket Books 1976)

Daniel P. Mannix, *Memoirs of a Sword Swallower* (San Francisco: V/Search Publications, 1950)

Stuart Rosenthal and Judith M. Kass, *The Hollywood Professionals IV: Todd Browning and Don Siegel* (London: The Tantivy Press, 1975)

David J. Skal and Elias Savada, *Dark Carnival: The Secret World of Tod Browning, Hollywood's Master of the Macabre* (New York: Anchor Books 1995)

Francois Couperin: *The Complete Masses*, James Tibbles, artist and author of liner notes (Paladino Music, 2012) (CD)

John Eckhardt, Jr., *Autobiography of Johnny Eck* (unpublished)

www.ingramcontent.com/pod-product-compliance
Lightning Source LLC
Chambersburg PA
CBHW072017150726
47999CB00002B/714